SUSHI

Full of delicious authentic recipes

SUSHI

Full of delicious authentic recipes

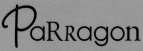

Bath New York Singapore Hong Kong Cologne Delhi Melbourne

This edition published by Parragon in 2008

Parragon Publishing
Queen Street House
4 Queen Street
Bath BA1 1HE, UK

Copyright © Parragon Books Ltd 2004

ISBN: 978-1-4075-2087-2
Printed in China

Produced by the Bridgewater Book Company Ltd

Notes for the Reader

This book uses imperial, metric, or US cup measurements. Follow the same units of measurement throughout; do not mix imperial and metric. All spoon measurements are level: teaspoons are assumed to be 5 ml, and tablespoons are assumed to be 15 ml.Unless otherwise stated, milk is assumed to be whole, eggs and individual vegetables such as potatoes are medium, and pepper is freshly ground black pepper.

The times given are an approximate guide only. Preparation times differ according to the techniques used by different people and the cooking times may also vary from those given as a result of the type of oven used. Optional ingredients, variations or serving sugggestions have not been included in the calculations.

Recipes using raw or very lightly cooked eggs should be avoided by infants, the elderly, pregnant woman, convalescents, and anyone with a chronic condition. Pregnant and breastfeeding women are advised to avoid eating peanuts and peanut products. Sufferers from nut allergies should be aware that some of the ready-prepared ingredients used in the recipes in this book may contain nuts. Always check the packaging before use.

Picture acknowledgement

The Bridgewater Book Company would like to thank Taesam Do/Foodpix/Getty Images for permission to reproduce copyright material for the endpapers.

Introduction 6

Rolling Your Own 8

Pressed and Scattered Sushi 30

It's a Wrap 52

Sushi Lounge 74

Index 96

Introduction

SUSHI IS ESSENTIALLY A SELECTION OF TOPPINGS, TRADITIONALLY RAW FISH, PRESSED ONTO SEASONED RICE. BUT AS ANYONE WHO LOVES SUSHI KNOWS, IN PRACTICE IT IS MUCH MORE THAN THAT. IT IS GREAT TO LOOK AT, DELICIOUS TO EAT, AND PLEASURABLE TO MAKE. MODERN SUSHI DOES NOT HAVE TO BE MADE FROM RAW FISH; COOKED FISH, MEATS, VEGETABLES, AND EGGS ARE ALL USED TO MAKE A RANGE OF COLORFUL, INTERESTING, AND INNOVATIVE TOPPINGS AND FILLINGS.

MAKING SUSHI REQUIRES A LITTLE PRACTICE; HOWEVER IT IS ACTUALLY MUCH EASIER THAN IT LOOKS. YOU DON'T NEED LOTS OF EQUIPMENT, BUT IF YOU HAVE ACCESS TO A JAPANESE STORE OR A GOOD KITCHEN STORE THEN YOU CAN BUY A SPECIAL BAMBOO MIXING TUB *(HANGIRI* OR *SUSHI-OKE)*, PRESSING BOX *(OSHI WAKU)*, AND RICE SPATULA *(SHAMOJI)*, THOUGH NONE ARE ESSENTIAL. ALL YOU REALLY NEED IS A SUSHI MAT *(MAKISU)*.

Sushi essentials

RAW FISH FOR SUSHI

Sushi is traditionally made using both raw and cooked fish. If you would like to make sushi with raw fish you must realize that this will add an element of risk to your eating experience. Raw fish is more likely to contain bacteria and parasites than cooked fish because it has not been subjected to the required amount of heat to kill them off. Freezing and then thawing raw fish may eliminate some problems but it will not make the fish completely safe, nor will it benefit the texture and flavor. All of the sushi recipes in this book can be made with cooked fish. If you prefer to use raw fish, then you should follow the guidelines below.

People with certain diseases (such as diabetes or liver disease) or weakened immune systems should never eat raw fish or shellfish. Levels of mercury, which is found in water from naturally occurring sources as well as industrial pollution, tend to be higher in long-lived, larger fish with darker meat, such as swordfish, king mackerel, and tuna. The elderly and pregnant women (along with nursing mothers and young children) should avoid eating these types of fish.

BUYING RAW FISH

You must be particularly careful when buying raw fish; it needs to be as fresh as possible and come from a reputable supplier. Fish should only be bought from a supplier or store that sells "sushi grade" or "sashimi grade" fish. This fish is often precut into blocks so that all you have to do is slice it into the required sizes. Buy shellfish that has come from certified waters. Once you have bought your fish you will need to take it straight home in a cold bag with some ice (usually available from the supplier) and put it in the refrigerator immediately. Use it on the day that you buy it.

PREPARING RAW FISH

Once you start your recipe, it is very important to prepare everything else before you take the fish out of the refrigerator, then use it quickly, and put the finished sushi back in the refrigerator as soon as it is made. Keep everything scrupulously clean. Take your sushi out of the refrigerator just before serving and don't leave it to sit out for any length of time. Hand plates round rather than putting them out for people to help themselves. Ideally, make the sushi at the last minute and serve it straightaway.

HOW TO TELL IF FISH AND SHELLFISH IS FRESH (APPLICABLE TO BOTH RAW AND COOKED):

• Look for firm flesh that bounces back when pressed.
• Fish eyes should be clear and shiny.
• Gills should be bright pink or red with no slime.
• The fish should smell like the ocean, not "fishy."
• Scales should be shiny and cling tightly to the skin.

• Shells of live clams, mussels, and oysters may be open but will close tightly when tapped.
• Live crabs and lobster will be moving.
• Shrimp will smell fresh.

HOW TO TELL IF FISH AND SHELLFISH IS PROPERLY COOKED:

• When cooked, fish flesh should be opaque and flake easily with a fork.
• Shrimp should turn pink and have white, firm flesh.
• Scallops turn an opaque white and firm up.
• Clams, mussels, and oysters are done when their shells open; throw away any that stay closed.

COMMON TYPES OF SUSHI AND SASHIMI GRADE FISH

maguro	tuna
toro	fatty tuna cut from the belly
hamachi	yellowtail
katsuo	bonito
saba	mackerel
sake	salmon
hirame	halibut
suzuki	sea bass
unagi	freshwater eel (this is sold cooked)
tako	octopus
ika	squid
awabi	abalone
kani	crab

Rolled sushi, or *maki-zushi*, is a very popular way of making sushi. Unlike finger sushi, which is quite hard to make well, rolled sushi needs only a little practice. A sheet of nori is spread with rice and fillings and rolled up. The roll can then be cut into bite-size pieces, which are served cut-side up so that you can see the filling. Sushi rolls can also be served whole if you prefer. They make a good lunchbox option for both adults and children if you wrap each roll in plastic wrap.

Rolled sushi is often filled with vegetables or pickles, pieces of cooked meat, chicken, or duck, cooked fish, or seafood. For children's sushi you can also use sticks of ham or cheese. Sushi rolls use only a small amount of filling, so you can choose quite expensive ingredients such as lobster and crab. You can also choose whether to make fat or thin rolls.

ROLLING YOUR OWN

Once you have made your rolls, you need to cut them with a very sharp, damp knife to stop the rice sticking. Traditionally sushi is dipped into Japanese soy sauce *(shoyu)*, but you can use mayonnaise or sweet chili sauce if you like. Rolled sushi makes a fantastic canapé or appetizer for a dinner party. Arrange the pieces of sushi on a rectangular plate and add a small pile of pickled ginger and wasabi to one corner.

ENOUGH FOR 24 PIECES

scant 1¼ cups sushi rice

scant 1½ cups water

1 piece of kombu (optional)

2 tbsp sushi rice seasoning

Sushi Rice

Rice is the most important ingredient in sushi. There are several brands of sushi rice on the market. All are white and short-grain, and marked specifically "sushi rice." If you can't find sushi rice, then use another type of short-grained white rice.

• Wash the sushi rice under cold running water until the water running through it is completely clear, then drain the rice. Put the rice in a pan with the water and the kombu, if you are using it, cover, and bring to a boil as quickly as you can. Remove the kombu, then turn the heat down and let simmer for 10 minutes. Turn off the heat and let the rice stand for 15 minutes. Do not at any point take the lid off the pan once you have removed the kombu.

• Put the hot rice in a *sushi-oke* (large, very shallow bowl) and pour the sushi rice seasoning evenly over the surface of the rice. Now you will need to use both hands, one to mix the seasoning into the rice with quick cutting strokes using a *shamoji* (spatula), and the other to fan the sushi rice in order to cool it down as quickly as you can. Mix the seasoning in carefully—you do not want to break a single rice grain.

• The sushi rice should look shiny and be at room temperature when you are ready to use it.

MAKES 24 PIECES

1 quantity freshly cooked Sushi Rice
6 small sheets of toasted nori
wasabi paste
½ ripe avocado, cut into thin sticks
6 crab sticks, split in half lengthwise
2-inch/5-cm piece of cucumber,
    peeled and cut into thin sticks

TO SERVE

shoyu (Japanese soy sauce)
pickled ginger

California Rolls

Crab sticks, sometimes called imitation crab sticks, are widely available. Made from fish or seafood, they are neatly shaped logs with a pink strip down one side.

Crab sticks are found in California rolls, but because of their neat shape they are also very useful for other types of rolled sushi.

• Divide the rice into 6 equal portions. Put a sheet of nori shiny-side down on a rolling mat with the longest end toward you and, using wet hands, spread 1 portion of the rice in an even layer on the nori, leaving ¾ inch/2 cm of nori visible at the end farthest away from you. Don't squash the rice or make the layer too thick—you should be able to see the nori through the rice.

• Spread a small amount of wasabi onto the rice at the end nearest you. Lay 2 thin avocado sticks down on top of the wasabi, keeping them parallel to the edge of the nori nearest you, then put 2 pieces of crab next to them. Add a line of thin cucumber sticks.

• To roll the sushi, fold the mat over, starting at the end where the ingredients are, and tucking in the end of the nori to start the roll. Keep rolling, lifting up the mat as you go and keeping the pressure even but gentle until you have finished the roll. Moisten the top edge of the nori with water to seal the sushi roll closed. Don't worry if anything falls out of the sides, just push it back in. The edges may well look ragged, but don't worry.

• Remove the roll from the mat and cut it into 4 even-size pieces with a wet, very sharp knife. If you don't use a sharp knife the roll will squash as you cut it. Arrange the rolls on a plate. Repeat with the remaining ingredients. Serve with shoyu, pickled ginger, and some extra wasabi paste.

MAKES 24 PIECES

6 asparagus spears

5½-oz/150-g piece of salmon fillet or
the same amount of sushi-grade
salmon, cut into thin sticks

1 tbsp oil

1 quantity freshly cooked Sushi Rice

6 small sheets of toasted nori

wasabi paste

1 tbsp Japanese mayonnaise

1 tsp toasted sesame seeds

TO SERVE

shoyu (Japanese soy sauce)

pickled ginger

Salmon, Asparagus, and Mayonnaise Rolls

Japanese mayonnaise is also called "kewpie mayonnaise" because of the kewpie doll logo used by the company. It usually comes in a plastic bottle within a bag printed with a kewpie doll outline. You can use ordinary mayonnaise instead, though whole egg mayonnaise will taste better because it tends to be less vinegary or sweet.

• Lay the asparagus flat in a skillet filled with simmering water and cook until tender when pierced with the tip of a knife. Cut into 3½-inch/9-cm lengths and let cool.

• If using the salmon fillet, pull the skin off and remove any bones. Heat the oil in a skillet and cook the salmon over medium heat on both sides for 8 minutes, or until it is cooked through. Let cool and flake into large pieces.

• Divide the rice into 6 equal portions. Put a sheet of nori shiny-side down on a rolling mat with the longest end toward you and, using wet hands, spread 1 portion of the rice in an even layer on the nori, leaving ¾ inch/2 cm of nori visible at the end farthest away from you.

• Spread a small amount of wasabi onto the rice at the end nearest you, then spread on the mayonnaise. Lay an asparagus spear on top of this, then put some of the salmon next to it. Sprinkle the sesame seeds on top.

• To roll the sushi, fold the mat over, starting at the end where the ingredients are, and tucking in the end of the nori to start the roll. Keep rolling, lifting up the mat as you go and keeping the pressure even but gentle until you have finished the roll. Moisten the top edge of the nori with water to seal the sushi roll closed.

• Remove the roll from the mat and cut it into 4 even-size pieces with a wet, very sharp knife. Turn the pieces on end and arrange them on a plate. Repeat with the remaining ingredients. Serve with shoyu, pickled ginger, and some extra wasabi paste.

MAKES 24 PIECES

6 asparagus spears

1 tbsp oil

6 shiitake mushrooms, sliced

1 quantity freshly cooked Sushi Rice

6 small sheets of toasted nori

wasabi paste

6 crab sticks, split in half lengthwise

PONZU SAUCE

3 tbsp mirin

2 tbsp rice vinegar

1 tbsp light soy sauce

2 tbsp bonito flakes

4 tbsp lemon juice

Crab, Asparagus, and Shiitake Rolls with Ponzu Sauce

Shiitake mushrooms can be bought both fresh and dried. If you can't find the fresh mushrooms, then soak dried ones in boiling water for 30 minutes, drain, and squeeze dry. You can now cook them according to the recipe.

• Lay the asparagus flat in a skillet filled with simmering water and cook until tender when pierced with the tip of a knife. Cut into 3½-inch/9-cm lengths and let cool.

• Heat the oil in a skillet and cook the mushrooms over medium heat for 5 minutes, or until completely soft.

• To make the Ponzu Sauce, put all the ingredients in a small pan and bring to a boil. Once they have boiled, turn off the heat, and cool the sauce.

• Divide the rice into 6 equal portions. Put a sheet of nori shiny-side down on a rolling mat with the longest end toward you and, using wet hands, spread 1 portion of the rice in an even layer on the nori, leaving ¾ inch/2 cm of nori visible at the end farthest away from you.

• Spread a small amount of wasabi onto the rice at the end nearest you. Lay an asparagus spear on top of the wasabi, then put 2 pieces of crab next to it. Add a line of mushrooms.

• To roll the sushi, fold the mat over, starting at the end where the ingredients are, and tucking in the end of the nori to start the roll. Keep rolling, lifting up the mat as you go and keeping the pressure even but gentle until you have finished the roll. Moisten the top edge of the nori with water to seal the sushi roll closed.

• Remove the roll from the mat and cut it into 4 even-size pieces with a wet, very sharp knife. Arrange the rolls on a plate. Repeat with the remaining ingredients and serve with the Ponzu Sauce.

MAKES 24 PIECES

5½-oz/150-g piece of salmon fillet

sichimi togarashi (seven-spice
  powder)

red pepper flakes

1 tbsp oil

1 quantity freshly cooked Sushi Rice

6 small sheets of toasted nori

2 tbsp Japanese mayonnaise

TO SERVE

shoyu (Japanese soy sauce)

wasabi paste

pickled ginger

Seven-Spiced Salmon Rolls

Sichimi togarashi
is a seven-spice mix
usually containing red
bell pepper, sansho
pepper, sesame seeds,
flax seeds, poppy seeds,
ground nori, and dried,
ground tangerine peel.

• Pull the skin off the salmon fillet and remove any bones. Dust the surface heavily with sichimi togarashi and sprinkle over a few red pepper flakes. Heat the oil in a skillet and cook the salmon over medium heat on both sides for 8 minutes, or until it is cooked through. Let cool and flake into large pieces.

• Divide the rice into 6 equal portions. Put a sheet of nori shiny-side down on a rolling mat with the longest end toward you and, using wet hands, spread 1 portion of the rice in an even layer on the nori, leaving ¾ inch/2 cm of nori visible at the end farthest away from you. Don't squash the rice or make the layer too thick—you should be able to see the nori through the rice.

• Spread the mayonnaise onto the rice at the end nearest you. Lay a sixth of the salmon on top of the mayonnaise.

• To roll the sushi, fold the mat over, starting at the end where the ingredients are, and tucking in the end of the nori to start the roll. Keep rolling, lifting up the mat as you go and keeping the pressure even but gentle until you have finished the roll. Moisten the top edge of the nori with water to seal the sushi roll closed.

• Remove the roll from the mat and cut it into 4 even-size pieces with a wet, very sharp knife. Turn the pieces on end and arrange them on a plate. Repeat with the remaining ingredients. Serve with shoyu, wasabi, and pickled ginger.

MAKES 24 PIECES

2 tbsp flour

1 egg, lightly beaten

4 tbsp tonkatsu crumbs or dried
white bread crumbs

7 oz/200 g pork fillet, cut into
thin slices

4 tbsp oil

1 quantity freshly cooked Sushi Rice

6 small sheets of toasted nori

2 tbsp Japanese mayonnaise

TO SERVE

shoyu (Japanese soy sauce)

wasabi paste

pickled ginger

Pork Tonkatsu Rolls

Tonkatsu crumbs are toasted bread crumbs, also called "panko," which are used for coating pork fillets before cooking them. They absorb less grease than normal bread crumbs, but you can use commercial pretoasted bread crumbs instead.

• Put the flour, egg, and crumbs in separate bowls. One by one, dust each piece of pork in the flour, dip it in the egg, then finally press it into the crumbs. Lay the breaded pork on a plate and let chill for 20 minutes.

• Heat the oil in a skillet and cook the pork on both sides until the crumbs are a golden brown. It won't take long as the slices are quite thin. Cut the slices into strips.

• Divide the rice into 6 equal portions. Put a sheet of nori shiny-side down on a rolling mat with the longest end toward you and, using wet hands, spread 1 portion of the rice in an even layer on the nori, leaving ¾ inch/2 cm of nori visible at the end farthest away from you.

• Spread the mayonnaise onto the rice at the end nearest you. Lay a sixth of the pork strips on top of the mayonnaise in a line.

• To roll the sushi, fold the mat over, starting at the end where the ingredients are, and tucking in the end of the nori to start the roll. Keep rolling, lifting up the mat as you go and keeping the pressure even but gentle until you have finished the roll. Moisten the top edge of the nori with water to seal the sushi roll closed.

• Remove the roll from the mat and cut it into 4 even-size pieces with a wet, very sharp knife. Turn the pieces on end and arrange them on a plate. Repeat with the remaining ingredients. Serve with shoyu, wasabi, and pickled ginger.

MAKES 24 PIECES

1 chicken breast, cut into strips

2 tbsp teriyaki sauce

1 tbsp oil

1 quantity freshly cooked Sushi Rice

6 small sheets of toasted nori

2-inch/5-cm piece of cucumber,
    peeled and cut into thin sticks

TO SERVE

shoyu (Japanese soy sauce)

wasabi paste

pickled ginger

Chicken Teriyaki Rolls

Teriyaki sauce is a widely available flavoring, or cook-in sauce. It is made from soy sauce, mirin, sake, sugar, and ginger, and gives food a glossy coating.

• Preheat the broiler to its highest setting. Toss the chicken in the teriyaki sauce, then the oil, and lay out on a foil-lined broiler pan. Broil the chicken strips on both sides for 4 minutes, put into a bowl with any cooking juices, and let cool.

• Divide the rice into 6 equal portions. Put a sheet of nori shiny-side down on a rolling mat with the longest end toward you and, using wet hands, spread 1 portion of the rice in an even layer on the nori, leaving ¾ inch/2 cm of nori visible at the end farthest away from you. Don't squash the rice or make the layer too thick—you should be able to see the nori through the rice.

• Lay the chicken strips in an even line onto the rice at the end nearest you. Add a line of thin cucumber sticks.

• To roll the sushi, fold the mat over, starting at the end where the ingredients are, and tucking in the end of the nori to start the roll. Keep rolling, lifting up the mat as you go and keeping the pressure even but gentle until you have finished the roll. Moisten the top edge of the nori with water to seal the sushi roll closed. Don't worry if anything falls out of the sides, just push it back in. The edges may well look ragged, but don't worry.

• Remove the roll from the mat and cut it into 4 even-size pieces with a wet, very sharp knife. Turn the pieces on end and arrange them on a plate. Repeat with the remaining ingredients. Serve with shoyu, wasabi, and pickled ginger.

MAKES 6

1 quantity freshly cooked Sushi Rice
6 small sheets of toasted nori
1 tbsp Japanese mayonnaise
1 tsp lemon zest
12 cooked jumbo shrimp, shelled
  and deveined

2 ripe avocados, cut into strips
2-inch/5-cm piece of cucumber,
  peeled and cut into thin sticks
6 bamboo skewers

Shrimp and Avocado Skewers

Nori sheets are made from dried laver seaweed and come in different sizes. If, however, you can only find one size, simply adjust the recipe to suit the size of the sheet. Buy nori sheets that are marked "toasted" if possible. Untoasted sheets are not as crisp or highly flavored, but you can toast them by passing the non-shiny side over a naked flame. When rolling the sheets, always put them on the mat shiny-side down.

• Divide the rice into 6 equal portions. Put a sheet of nori shiny-side down on a rolling mat with the longest end toward you and, using wet hands, spread 1 portion of the rice in an even layer on the nori, leaving ¾ inch/2 cm of nori visible at the end farthest away from you. Don't squash the rice or make the layer too thick—you should be able to see the nori through the rice.

• Mix the mayonnaise with the lemon zest and spread some onto the rice at the end nearest to you. Lay 2 shrimp end to end on top of the mayonnaise, then put a line of avocado next to them. Lay a line of cucumber sticks next to the avocado.

• To roll the sushi, fold the mat over, starting at the end where the ingredients are, and tucking in the end of the nori to start the roll. Keep rolling, lifting up the mat as you go and keeping the pressure even but gentle until you have finished the roll. Moisten the top edge of the nori with water to seal the sushi roll closed. Don't worry if anything falls out of the sides, just push it back in. The edges may well look ragged, but don't worry.

• Remove the roll from the mat and cut into 4 even-size pieces with a wet, very sharp knife. If you don't use a sharp knife the roll will squash as you cut it. Lay the pieces on their side. Push each bamboo skewer through 4 pieces, making sure they are at the end so that you can eat them easily.

MAKES 24 PIECES

1 quantity freshly cooked Sushi Rice

6 small sheets of toasted nori

¼ ripe avocado, cut into strips

2-inch/5-cm piece of cucumber,
    peeled and cut into thin sticks

6 crab sticks, split in half lengthwise

3 tbsp toasted sesame seeds

Inside-Out California Rolls

Sesame seeds are available raw and toasted, the toasted ones having a more pronounced flavor. If you can only find raw ones, then dry-fry them in a hot skillet until they brown and start to smell aromatic.

• Divide the rice into 6 equal portions. Line a rolling mat with plastic wrap to prevent the rice sticking to it. Put a sheet of nori shiny-side down on the mat with the longest end toward you. Using wet hands, spread 1 portion of the rice in an even layer on the nori, leaving no gaps, then turn the nori over so that the mat is against the rice.

• Put some avocado in a layer at one end of the roll, keeping it parallel to the edge nearest you, and lay 2 pieces of crab in a line beside it. Put a line of cucumber next to them.

• To roll the sushi, fold the mat over, starting at the end where the ingredients are, and tucking in the end of the nori to start the roll. Keep rolling, lifting up the mat as you go and keeping the pressure even but gentle until you have finished the roll. Put the sesame seeds on a plate and roll the sushi in them to coat the rice.

• Remove the roll from the mat and cut it into 4 even-size pieces with a wet, very sharp knife. If you don't use a sharp knife the roll will squash as you cut it. Turn the pieces on end and arrange them on a plate. Repeat with the remaining ingredients.

MAKES 24 PIECES

5½ oz/150 g tenderloin steak, trimmed

2 tbsp teriyaki sauce

1 tbsp oil

1 quantity freshly cooked Sushi Rice

6 small sheets of toasted nori

2 scallions, shredded

3 tbsp toasted sesame seeds

Inside-Out Rolls with Beef Teriyaki

This recipe works equally well with chicken, salmon, or slices of tofu. Use the same weight of any of the above and follow the recipe in the same way.

• Beat the steak out flat using a meat mallet or rolling pin to make it thinner and more tender. Coat the steak in the teriyaki sauce and let it marinate for an hour. Heat the oil in a skillet and cook the steak for 3 minutes on each side. Cut the steak into thin strips.

• Divide the rice into 6 equal portions. Line a rolling mat with plastic wrap to prevent the rice sticking to it. Put a sheet of nori shiny-side down on the mat with the longest end toward you and, using wet hands, spread 1 portion of the rice in an even layer on the nori, leaving no gaps, then turn the nori over so that the mat is against the rice. Put a sixth of the beef teriyaki in a layer at one long end of the roll, top with a layer of scallion, and sprinkle with a few sesame seeds.

• To roll the sushi, fold the mat over, starting at the end where the ingredients are, and tucking in the end of the nori to start the roll. Keep rolling, lifting up the mat as you go and keeping the pressure even but gentle until you have finished the roll. Put the remaining sesame seeds on a plate and roll the sushi in them to coat the rice.

• Remove the roll from the mat and cut it into 4 even-size pieces with a wet, very sharp knife. If you don't use a sharp knife the roll will squash as you cut it. Turn the pieces on end and arrange them on a plate. Repeat with the remaining ingredients.

These are the two easiest styles of sushi to make as they involve no rolling or shaping by hand. Pressed sushi and box sushi, *oshi-zushi* and *hako-zushi*, are made in a three-piece bamboo pressing box called an *oshi waku*, but a loose-bottom cake pan or terrine pan with drop-down sides will work just as well. If you only have fixed-bottom pans, then make the sushi upside-down, putting the toppings into the bottom of the pan, pressing the rice on top, then simply turning the sushi out. If you arrange your toppings in diagonal strips and cut the sushi into bar shapes, you will end up with an interesting striped effect. Once you have turned the sushi out, wait for a few minutes before cutting it to allow the flavors to develop. You will need to use a very sharp knife, wiped with a damp cloth between each cut, to keep it neat.

PRESSED AND SCATTERED SUSHI

Scattered sushi, *chirashi-zushi*, is sometimes called "housewives' sushi" because this is the type most commonly made at home in Japan. All you need to make this is an attractive serving bowl for each person eating it. Red and black lacquered wooden bowls look wonderful, but you can use any bowl. Some suggested toppings are given in this chapter, but you can treat scattered sushi as you would a rice salad and mix and match the toppings as you like. You can add some pickled ginger and wasabi to the topping as a garnish or serve them separately in little bowls alongside some soy sauce and mayonnaise for dipping.

MAKES 8–10 PIECES
½ quantity freshly cooked Sushi Rice
2 tbsp Japanese mayonnaise
2 tsp lemon zest
5½ oz/150 g smoked salmon
1 large ripe avocado, cut into
    thin sticks

TO SERVE
pickled ginger
wasabi paste

Salmon, Lemon Mayonnaise, and Avocado Pressed Sushi Bars

Oshi waku are wooden boxes made for pressing sushi. They consist of a frame plus a removable lid and base and come in different sizes.

• Oil an *oshi waku* or terrine pan (preferably with drop-down sides) and line it with a piece of plastic wrap so that the plastic wrap hangs over the edges. This is to help you pull the sushi out afterward. Pack the pan 1¼ inches/ 3 cm full with the rice. Mix the mayonnaise with the lemon zest and spread a layer of mayonnaise on top of the rice. Arrange the smoked salmon and avocado in thick, diagonal strips on top of the rice. Cover the top of the rice with a strip of plastic wrap, put another terrine pan on top, and add something heavy, such as a couple of cans of tomatoes, to weigh it down.

• Let the sushi chill for 15 minutes, then take off the pan and weights and pull out the sushi. Cut the sushi into 8–10 pieces with a wet, sharp knife. Serve with pickled ginger and wasabi paste.

MAKES 15 PIECES

7 oz/200 g sushi-grade tuna
or tuna fillet, thinly sliced

2 tbsp teriyaki sauce

1 tbsp oil

10 green beans, trimmed and
cut in half

oil, for cooking

1 tsp toasted sesame seeds

½ quantity freshly cooked Sushi Rice

2 tbsp Japanese mayonnaise

TO SERVE

pickled ginger

wasabi paste

Teriyaki Tuna Pressed Sushi with Green Bean Strips

Pickled ginger slices are used to cleanse the palate in between eating different types of sushi. Pickled ginger can be bought in bags and is often a bright pink color.

• Coat the tuna slices in the teriyaki sauce and cook in the oil in a skillet for 1 minute on each side. Then cut them into thick strips. Blanch the green beans in boiling water for a minute, then cool under cold running water and drain.

• Oil an *oshi waku* or 7-inch/18-cm loose-bottom square cake pan and line it with a piece of plastic wrap so that the plastic wrap hangs over the edges. This is to help you pull the sushi out afterward. Oil the plastic wrap and sprinkle in the sesame seeds. Pack the pan 1¼ inches/3 cm full with the rice. Spread a layer of mayonnaise on top. Arrange the tuna and beans in diagonal strips on top of the rice. Cover the top of the rice with a strip of plastic wrap, put another cake pan on top, and weight down with something heavy, such as a couple of cans of tomatoes.

• Let the sushi chill for 15 minutes, then take off the pan and weights, loosen the sides of the pan, and pull out the sushi. Cut the sushi into about 15 pieces with a wet, sharp knife. Serve with pickled ginger and wasabi paste.

MAKES 8–10 PIECES

½ quantity freshly cooked Sushi Rice

2 tbsp Japanese mayonnaise

7 oz/200 g smoked salmon

½ cucumber, peeled and cut into
    very thin slices

TO GARNISH

2 lemons, cut into wedges

handful of mint sprigs

Pressed Sushi Bars with
Smoked Salmon and Cucumber

Smoked salmon makes a good ingredient in sushi because of its texture. You can buy a piece of fillet and slice it yourself if you want thicker slices.

• Oil an *oshi waku* or terrine pan (preferably with drop-down sides) and line it with a piece of plastic wrap so that the plastic wrap hangs over the edges. This is to help you pull the sushi out afterward. Pack the pan 1¼ inches/ 3 cm full with the rice. Spread a layer of mayonnaise on top of the rice. Arrange the smoked salmon and cucumber in diagonal strips on top of the rice, doubling up the smoked salmon layers if you have enough so that the topping is nice and thick. Cover the top of the rice with a strip of plastic wrap, put another terrine pan on top, and add something heavy, such as a couple of cans of tomatoes, to weight it down.

• Let the sushi chill for 15 minutes, then take off the pan and weights and pull out the sushi. Cut the sushi into 8–10 pieces with a wet, sharp knife. Garnish with lemon wedges and mint sprigs.

MAKES 15 PIECES
½ quantity freshly cooked Sushi Rice
2 tbsp Japanese mayonnaise
1 tsp toasted sesame seeds
½ avocado, cut into strips

4 crab sticks, sliced on the diagonal,
   or the flesh from a cooked,
   prepared crab
½ cucumber, peeled and cut into
   very thin slices

TO GARNISH
lemon quarters
dill

TO SERVE
pickled ginger
wasabi paste

Pressed California Sushi

Wasabi is usually bought as a paste or powder and is made from a grated root. The powder can be mixed to a paste and is often of a better quality than the tubes of paste. Wasabi gets rid of any fishiness in sushi, but it is very strong so be careful not to use too much.

• Oil an *oshi waku* or 7-inch/18-cm loose-bottom square cake pan and line it with a piece of plastic wrap so that the plastic wrap hangs over the edges. This is to help you pull the sushi out afterward. Pack the pan 1¼ inches/3 cm full with the rice. Spread a layer of mayonnaise on top of the rice and sprinkle over the sesame seeds. Arrange the avocado, crab, and cucumber in thick, diagonal strips on top of the rice. Cover the top of the rice with a strip of plastic wrap, put another cake pan on top, and add something heavy, such as a couple of cans of tomatoes, to weight it down.
• Chill the sushi for 15 minutes, then take off the pan and weights, loosen the sides of the pan, and pull out the sushi. Cut the sushi into about 15 pieces with a wet, sharp knife. Garnish with lemon and dill and serve with pickled ginger and a dab of wasabi paste.

MAKES 15 PIECES
2 red bell peppers
½ quantity freshly cooked Sushi Rice
oil, for brushing
4 sundried tomatoes in oil, drained
   and cut into strips

3½ oz/100 g mozzarella, cut into
   thin slices
handful of small basil leaves

Mediterranean Pressed Sushi

Weigh down pressed sushi by applying a firm, even pressure so that the decorative layer stays flat. The ingredients can be arranged in the bottom and the rice pressed on top, or the other way round.

• Preheat the oven to 400°F/200°C. Put the bell peppers in a roasting pan and cook them for 30 minutes, or until the skins have browned and started to puff away from the flesh. Let cool, then pull off the skins. Cut each bell pepper in half and discard the stalk, seeds, and membrane. Cut the bell peppers into strips.

• Oil an *oshi waku* or 7-inch/18-cm loose-bottom square cake pan and line it with a piece of plastic wrap so that the plastic wrap hangs over the edges. This is to help you pull the sushi out afterward. Pack the pan 1¼ inches/3 cm full with the rice and brush the top with a tiny amount of oil to help the toppings stick.

• Arrange the bell pepper and mozzarella in thick, diagonal strips on top of the rice, alternating basil leaves and sundried tomatoes as thinner strips between the thick pepper and mozzarella strips. Cover the top of the rice with a strip of plastic wrap, put another pan or flat tray on top and add something heavy, such as a couple of cans of tomatoes, to weight it down.

• Let the sushi chill for 15 minutes, then take off the pan and weights, loosen the sides of the pan, and pull out the sushi. Cut the sushi into about 15 pieces with a wet, sharp knife.

SERVES 4

8 snow peas

2-inch/5-cm piece of daikon

1 quantity freshly cooked Sushi Rice

juice and zest of 1 lemon

2 scallions, finely chopped

2 smoked mackerel, skin removed
    and cut into diagonal strips

½ cucumber, peeled and
    cut into slices

TO GARNISH

pickled ginger

strips of toasted nori

wasabi paste

Scattered Sushi with Smoked Mackerel

Daikon is a long,
white radish that has a
crisp white flesh and a
peppery flavor. It goes
well with fish and is
often used as a garnish.

• Cook the snow peas in boiling, salted water for 1 minute. Drain and put aside to cool. Shred the daikon using the finest setting on a mandoline or a very sharp knife. If you are using a knife, then cut the daikon into long, thin slices and cut each slice along its length as finely as you can.

• Mix the sushi rice with the lemon juice and lemon zest.

• Divide the rice between 4 wooden or ceramic bowls—they should be about ¾ inch/2 cm full. Sprinkle the scallion over the top. Arrange the mackerel, cucumber, snow peas, and daikon on top of the rice. Garnish with pickled ginger, nori strips, and a small mound of wasabi.

SERVES 4

8 dried shiitake mushrooms

2-inch/5-cm piece of daikon, peeled

2-inch/5-cm piece of carrot, peeled

1 tbsp soy sauce

1 tsp mirin

1 tsp brown sugar

7 oz/200 g tenderloin steak, trimmed

1 quantity freshly cooked Sushi Rice

TO GARNISH

strips of toasted nori

wasabi paste

TO SERVE

pickled ginger

Scattered Sushi with Soy-Glazed Steak

Mirin is a sweet rice wine that acts as a flavoring. It is used to make sushi rice and gives a lustre to the rice as well as adding flavor. Hon mirin and shin mirin are the 2 varieties, the difference being that hon mirin contains more alcohol.

• Soak the mushrooms in boiling water for 20 minutes, then simmer them in the same liquid for 3 minutes. Lift them out and squeeze them dry. Chop 4 mushrooms into small pieces and halve the rest. Shred the daikon and carrot using the finest setting on a mandoline or a very sharp knife. If you are using a knife, then cut the daikon and carrot into long, thin slices and cut each slice along its length as finely as you can.

• Preheat the broiler to its highest setting. Mix the soy sauce, mirin, and brown sugar together and brush the mixture all over the steak. Broil the steak for 3 minutes on each side, then let it rest for a minute. Slice into strips.

• Mix the sushi rice with the chopped shiitake mushrooms.

• Fill 1 large or 4 small wooden or ceramic bowls or plates with the rice—they should be about ¾ inch/2 cm full. Arrange the steak and halved mushrooms on top of the rice and add a neat pile of shredded daikon and carrot to each bowl. Garnish with some nori strips and a small mound of wasabi. Serve the pickled ginger on the side.

SERVES 4

6 large raw shrimp, shelled
   and deveined

1 tbsp oil

1 cooked prepared crab

1 quantity freshly cooked Sushi Rice

juice and zest of 1 lemon

1 ripe avocado, cut into strips

½ cucumber, peeled and cut
   into slices

Scattered Sushi with Shrimp, Crab, and Avocado

If you would like to keep
the shrimp straight so that
they are easier to arrange in
lines, then push a skewer
through their length before
cooking to stop them
curling up.

• Cook the shrimp by sautéing them for 2 minutes on each side in the oil. Once they are cooked, let cool, then cut in half lengthwise. Lift the crabmeat out of the shell.

• Mix the sushi rice with the lemon juice and lemon zest.

• Divide the rice between 4 wooden or ceramic bowls—they should be about ¾ inch/2 cm full. Arrange the shrimp, crab, avocado, and cucumber on top of the rice.

SERVES 4

1 cooked lobster

2 tbsp Japanese mayonnaise

1 tsp wasabi paste

1 quantity freshly cooked Sushi Rice

1 tbsp pickled ginger,
   very finely chopped

½ cucumber, cut into slices

1 ripe avocado, cut into slices

TO GARNISH

wasabi paste

pickled ginger

Scattered Sushi with Lobster and Wasabi Mayonnaise

Lobster can be bought cooked, but if you plan on cooking it yourself then make sure that you buy it live.

• Take the meat out of the lobster shell in as big pieces as you can. If your lobster is whole, the best way to do this is to twist off the head and halve the body down the center with a big sharp knife or cleaver. The claws will have to be smashed open to get at the meat. Cover them with a cloth and hit them hard with a rolling pin.

• Mix the mayonnaise with the wasabi. Mix the sushi rice with the finely chopped pickled ginger.

• Divide the rice between 4 wooden or ceramic bowls—they should be about ¾ inch/2 cm full. Arrange the lobster, cucumber, and avocado on top of the rice and drizzle the wasabi mayonnaise into the gaps. Garnish with pickled ginger and a small mound of wasabi.

MAKES 8 SHELLS

8 scallops with their shells
1 tbsp oil
juice and zest of ½ lime
⅓ quantity freshly cooked Sushi Rice
handful of fresh cilantro leaves

TO GARNISH

pickled ginger
wasabi paste
3 tbsp Japanese mayonnaise

Cocktail Scattered Sushi on Scallop Shells

Scallops can be bought on the shell and the fish store may even be able to clean them for you. Packages of scallop shells can also be bought for decorative purposes.

• Remove the scallops from their shells and clean and keep the shells for serving. Clean the scallops by pulling off the small, white, shiny muscle and its membrane. Leave the roe attached, but check to see if there is a black vein that needs to be cut off—this is easiest with a pair of scissors. Heat the oil in a skillet and briefly sauté the scallops on both sides until they are lightly browned and cooked through. Squeeze a little of the lime juice over each scallop and let cool.

• Mix the sushi rice with the remaining lime juice and zest.

• Divide the rice between 8 scallop shells—make a small, neat mound on each one and flatten the top a little. Arrange a scallop along with a few cilantro leaves on top of the rice in each shell, then garnish with a piece of pickled ginger, a tiny mound of wasabi, and a spoonful of mayonnaise. Serve on a platter with a pile of chopsticks.

Hand-rolled sushi, *temaki*, make perfect snacks. They are big enough to need more than one bite and are reasonably filling. Boat sushi, *gunkanmaki*, make a nice addition to a sushi platter as they vary the shapes you are using.

Legend has it that hand rolls were invented so that Japanese gangsters could eat while they were playing cards. The rolls are designed to be eaten with your hands and are very easy to pick up. They are best made at the last minute so that the nori stays crisp. Hand rolls can be served ready-made or, if you prefer, you can serve up the rice and fillings in bowls. Give each one of your guests a pile of nori squares and let them roll up their own. It is best to put a smear of wasabi and a few drops of soy into the roll before you eat it as they are hard to dip successfully. Mini hand rolls using smaller nori squares make good canapés.

IT'S A WRAP

Boat sushi are made by wrapping a piece of nori round a molded piece of rice. They are the best shape of sushi for serving toppings such as fish roe or slightly softer mixtures such as tuna mayonnaise or egg mayonnaise. Ready-made sandwich fillings or salad toppings are also good fillings for these and the rice base will absorb any excess sauce. You can vary the size of boat sushi, but pieces that take one or two bites are best.

MAKES 6 PIECES

5½-oz/150-g piece of salmon fillet,
    skin on

salt and pepper

1 tbsp oil

¼ quantity freshly cooked Sushi Rice

3 large sheets of toasted nori, halved

2 scallions, halved and shredded

4 tbsp Japanese mayonnaise

2 tbsp sweet chili sauce

TO SERVE

thin cucumber sticks

Sweet Chili Salmon Hand Rolls

Sweet chili sauce is available in many different brands. The best are Thai brands, available from Chinese and Thai stores.

• Season the piece of salmon with the salt and pepper. Heat the oil in a skillet until it is very hot, then add the salmon skin-side down. Cook for 2 minutes until the skin is very crisp, then turn the heat down to medium and cook for an additional 2 minutes. Turn the salmon over and cook for an additional minute, or until it is cooked through. Let cool, then flake the salmon, keeping some pieces attached to the crispy skin.

• Lay a piece of nori out on the counter and put some rice on the sheet. Spread the rice out evenly so that it takes up the bottom two-thirds of the sheet. Lay a sixth of the salmon, salmon skin, and scallion on the rice, then drizzle over a little mayonnaise and dot on a tiny amount of sweet chili sauce. Roll the nori into a cone, folding the bottom corner in as you roll. You will have to paste the join together with a couple of crushed grains of rice. Repeat with the other pieces of nori. Garnish with cucumber.

MAKES 6 PIECES

12 squid rings

4 tbsp all-purpose flour

1 tsp Szechuan pepper or black
pepper, crushed

1 tsp sea salt, crushed

oil, for cooking

3 large sheets of toasted nori, halved

¼ quantity freshly cooked Sushi Rice

4 tbsp Japanese mayonnaise

Salt and Pepper Squid Hand Rolls

Szechuan pepper is not a real pepper, but is made from the red berries of the prickly ash tree. The Japanese version is called sansho and is interchangeable.

• Pull any membranes off the squid rings, then cut each one in half. Mix the flour with the Szechuan pepper and salt and put it with the squid in a plastic bag. Shake well until the squid is thoroughly coated.

• Heat about ¾ inch/2 cm of oil in a wok until it is very hot, then add the squid in batches and cook, stirring, for a minute, or until the coating is browned. Drain on paper towels to get rid of any excess oil.

• Lay a piece of nori out on the counter and put some rice on the sheet. Spread the rice out evenly so that it takes up the bottom two-thirds of the sheet. Lay a sixth of the salt and pepper squid on the rice, then drizzle over a little mayonnaise. Roll the nori into a cone, folding the bottom corner in as you roll. You will have to paste the join together with a couple of crushed grains of rice. Repeat with the other pieces of nori.

MAKES 6 PIECES

6 thin strips of cod or haddock

oil, for deep frying

3 large sheets of toasted nori, halved

¼ quantity freshly cooked Sushi Rice

3 tbsp tartar sauce, plus extra
to serve

3 scallions, halved and shredded

Cod Hand Rolls with Tartar Sauce

Tartar sauce can be easily bought, just look for a premium brand based on a whole egg mayonnaise for the best flavor. If you don't like tartar sauce, then use mayonnaise with this recipe.

• Deep-fry the cod strips until golden brown. Let cool, then cut into 1½-inch/4-cm pieces.

• Lay a piece of nori out on the counter and put some rice on the sheet. Spread the rice out evenly so that it takes up the bottom two-thirds of the sheet. Spread a little of the tartar sauce onto the rice and top with a sixth of the cod pieces and scallion. Roll the nori into a cone, folding the bottom corner in as you roll. You will have to paste the join together with a couple of crushed grains of rice. Repeat with the other pieces of nori. Serve with extra tartar sauce for dipping.

MAKES 6 PIECES

¼ barbecued or Peking duck

4 tbsp hoisin or plum sauce

3 large sheets of toasted nori, halved

¼ quantity freshly cooked Sushi Rice

2 scallions, halved and shredded, plus

extra to garnish

Duck and Hoisin Hand Rolls

Barbecued duck can be bought from Chinese restaurants where you will see it hanging in the window. You can also buy it from supermarkets alongside the Chinese ready-meals. A roasted duck breast will also work for this recipe.

• Pull the flesh and skin off the duck in big pieces, then slice these into strips. If you have lots of skin, then just keep the crispiest bits. Get rid of any excess fat. Toss the duck flesh and skin with half the hoisin or plum sauce.

• Lay a piece of nori out on the counter and put some rice on the sheet. Spread the rice out evenly so that it takes up the bottom two-thirds of the sheet. Lay a sixth of the duck, duck skin, and scallion on the rice, then drizzle over a little more of the hoisin or plum sauce. Roll the nori into a cone, folding the bottom corner in as you roll. You will have to paste the join together with a couple of crushed grains of rice. Repeat with the other pieces of nori. Garnish with shredded scallions.

MAKES 6 PIECES

1 tsp black pepper

1 tbsp grated fresh gingerroot

1 tbsp sesame seeds

5½ oz/150 g sushi-grade tuna
   or very fresh tuna fillet

salt

2 tbsp oil

3 large sheets of toasted nori, halved

¼ quantity freshly cooked Sushi Rice

½ cucumber, cut into thin sticks

4 tbsp Japanese mayonnaise

wasabi paste

Tuna Tataki Hand Rolls

Hand rolls can be made in different sizes. They should ideally be big enough to need several bites, but you can make smaller cocktail-size rolls if you prefer.

• Mix the black pepper, ginger, and sesame seeds together and rub them all over the tuna, pressing the seeds on firmly. Season the tuna lightly with salt. Heat the oil in a skillet until it is very hot. Sear the tuna on all sides for 6 minutes, or until it is almost cooked through—keep pressing it until it feels firm. Remove from the skillet, let cool, then slice into thin slices.

• Lay out a piece of nori on the counter and put some rice on the sheet. Spread the rice out evenly so that it takes up the bottom two-thirds of the sheet. Lay a sixth of the tuna and cucumber on the rice, then drizzle over a little mayonnaise and dot on a tiny amount of wasabi. Roll the nori into a cone, folding the bottom corner in as you roll. You will have to paste the join together with a couple of crushed grains of rice. Repeat with the other pieces of nori.

MAKES 6 PIECES

½ cup soy sauce

2 tbsp mirin

2 tbsp sake

honey, to taste

3 large sheets of toasted nori, halved

¼ quantity freshly cooked Sushi Rice

2 smoked eel fillets, cut into strips
lengthwise

½ ripe avocado, cut into slices

Glazed Eel Hand Rolls

The eel *(unagi)* used for sushi has a soy, sake, and mirin glaze brushed over it before cooking. You can buy glazed eel from Japanese stores, or you can use smoked eel fillets, which may be easier to find.

• Put the soy sauce, mirin, and sake in a pan and let simmer for 5 minutes, or until slightly thickened. Stir in a teaspoon of honey, then taste, adding more honey until the sauce is sweet enough for you.

• Lay out a piece of nori on the counter and put some rice on the sheet. Spread the rice out evenly so that it takes up the bottom two-thirds of the sheet. Lay a sixth of the eel over the rice and drizzle the eel and rice liberally with the sauce. Add a couple of slices of avocado. Roll the nori into a cone, folding the bottom corner in as you roll. You will have to paste the join together with a couple of crushed grains of rice. Repeat with the other pieces of nori.

MAKES 8 PIECES
⅓ quantity freshly cooked Sushi Rice
2 small sheets of toasted nori, each
    cut into 4 strips lengthwise
wasabi paste
8 tbsp salmon, trout, or flying fish roe

TO SERVE
soy sauce
pickled ginger

Salmon Roe Sushi Boats

Roe is often used for
making sushi. Most roe
used is orange, either large
salmon or trout roe, or tiny
flying fish roe. It can be
bought in jars.

• Divide the rice into 8 batches. Dampen your hands to stop the rice sticking, then shape each batch of the rice into an oval using your hands. Carefully wrap a strip of nori round each piece of rice, trim off any excess, then stick together at the join using a couple of crushed grains of rice.
• Dab a little wasabi on top of each sushi boat and top with a tablespoon of the salmon roe. Serve the sushi straightaway with soy sauce and pickled ginger on the side.

MAKES 8 PIECES

20 green beans, trimmed
    and finely sliced
1 tbsp sesame oil
1 tbsp toasted sesame seeds
salt and pepper

1 tsp grated lemon zest
⅓ quantity freshly cooked Sushi Rice
2 small sheets of toasted nori, each
    cut into 4 strips lengthwise
wasabi paste

TO SERVE

soy sauce
pickled ginger

Green Bean Sushi Boats

Bean shredders are the best way to shred beans into long strips. They are small plastic frames filled with 5 or 6 blades.

• Put the green beans in a pan with a little water and bring to a boil. Cook for 2 minutes, then drain and toss with the sesame oil and sesame seeds. Season with salt and pepper to taste and mix in the lemon zest.

• Divide the rice into 8 batches. Dampen your hands to stop the rice sticking, then shape each batch into an oval using your hands. Carefully wrap a strip of nori round each piece of rice, trim off any excess, then stick together at the join using a couple of crushed grains of rice.

• Dab a little wasabi on top of each sushi boat and top with the green beans. Serve the sushi straightaway with soy sauce and pickled ginger on the side.

MAKES 8 PIECES

1/3 quantity freshly cooked Sushi Rice

2 small sheets of toasted nori, each
cut into 4 strips lengthwise

2 tbsp Japanese mayonnaise

1 tsp grated lemon zest

2 tsp lemon juice

2 scallions, finely chopped

1 smoked trout fillet, flaked

2 oz/55 g smoked salmon,
cut into strips

TO SERVE

Ponzu Sauce

4 radishes, finely chopped

Smoked Trout Sushi Boats

Smoked trout can be bought as fillets or as whole trout. The whole trout often have a more pronounced flavor.

• Divide the rice into 8 batches. Dampen your hands to stop the rice sticking, then shape each batch of the rice into an oval using your hands. Carefully wrap a strip of nori round each piece of rice, trim off any excess, then stick together at the join using a couple of crushed grains of rice.

• Mix the mayonnaise with the lemon zest and juice and spread a little on top of each sushi boat. Sprinkle with some scallion, then top with some of the smoked trout and smoked salmon. Serve the sushi straightaway with Ponzu Sauce and chopped radish.

MAKES 8 PIECES
1 small cooked prepared crab
1 tsp grated lemon zest
1 tsp black pepper
2 tbsp Japanese mayonnaise

salt
⅓ quantity freshly cooked Sushi Rice
2 small sheets of toasted nori, each
    cut into 4 strips lengthwise
juice of 1 lemon

TO GARNISH
2 lemons, cut into wedges

Lemon Pepper Crab Sushi Boats

To make a really quick and easy topping, use a can of lemon pepper tuna instead of the crab. Drain the can of any excess liquid and stir it well before use.

• Lift the crabmeat out of the shell and mix with the lemon, black pepper, and Japanese mayonnaise. Season with salt to taste.

• Divide the rice into 8 batches. Dampen your hands to stop the rice sticking, then shape each batch of the rice into an oval using your hands. Carefully wrap a strip of nori round each piece of rice, trim off any excess, then stick the seaweed together at the join using a couple of crushed grains of rice.

• Top each sushi boat with some of the crab mixture and squeeze over a few drops of lemon juice. Serve the sushi straightaway with lemon wedges on the side.

Sushi is becoming more and more inventive. Toppings are no longer restricted to raw fish and other Japanese-style ingredients; the traditional filling of rice is being replaced by noodles or even potato and egg; while red bell pepper and other ingredients are replacing the nori wrapping. Modern Japanese restaurants and sushi bars serve up new ideas on a daily basis and sushi appears on the menus of all sorts of other types of eating establishments. Sushi is no longer just Japanese, but is popular around the world. In fact, it has become part of the modern dining experience, and as such, the accompaniments it is served with have undergone a process of modernization too. Traditionally, hot or cold sake or green tea is served with sushi, and these two drinks go particularly well, but Japanese beer or wine also make a good companions.

SUSHI LOUNGE

This chapter contains a few extra dishes that are served at sushi bars. Tempura, which are crisp deep-fried fish, seafood, and vegetables, make a great accompaniment to sushi because they have a completely different texture and flavor. You can use any type of fish or seafood, as well as most firm-textured vegetables that cook through quickly. Tempura needs to be served hot, so make it at the last minute. Miso soup is a traditional accompaniment to sushi. You can serve it at the start of the meal, alongside the sushi, or as a refreshing palate cleanser at the end.

All these sushi recipes make good appetizers for dinner parties or canapés to serve with drinks. Mix and match a few of the recipes, plus a few from other chapters, to make up individual plates or a large sushi platter. Serve alongside miso in tiny cups for sipping.

MAKES 24 PIECES
4 oz/115 g sushi-grade tuna or piece
   of tuna fillet
1 tbsp oil
3½ oz/100 g soba noodles,
   broken into pieces
1 scallion, green part only,
   cut into thin slices

1 tbsp light soy sauce
½ tbsp rice wine vinegar
wasabi paste
1 tbsp pickled ginger, finely chopped
6 small sheets of toasted nori
½ cucumber, peeled and finely
   shredded

Soba Noodle Rolls

Soba noodles are long, brownish-gray noodles made from buckwheat and wheat flour. They can be eaten hot or cold, as here.

• If using a piece of tuna fillet, heat the oil in a skillet and sear the tuna on all sides for 6 minutes, or until it is almost cooked through. Cut the sushi or cooked tuna into strips.

• Cook the soba noodles in a pan of boiling water until they are just cooked through, drain, and rinse under cold running water. Drain thoroughly. Gently mix the soba noodles with the scallion, soy sauce, rice wine vinegar, a pinch of wasabi, and the pickled ginger.

• Divide the noodles into 6 equal portions. Put a sheet of nori shiny-side down on a rolling mat with the longest end toward you and mound 1 portion of the noodle mixture on the bottom third of the nori. Lay a sixth of the cucumber on top, then a layer of tuna strips.

• To roll the sushi, fold the mat over, starting at the end where the ingredients are, and tucking in the end of the nori to start the roll. Keep rolling, lifting up the mat as you go and keeping the pressure even but gentle until you have finished the roll. Moisten the top edge of the nori with water to seal the sushi roll closed. Don't worry if anything falls out of the sides, just push it back in.

• Remove the roll from the mat and cut it into 4 even-size pieces with a wet, very sharp knife. Turn the pieces on end and arrange them on a plate. Repeat the process with the remaining ingredients.

MAKES 24 PIECES
2 large potatoes, peeled and cut
    into quarters
1 scallion, finely chopped
wasabi paste
4 oz/115 g sushi-grade salmon
    or piece of salmon fillet

1 tbsp oil
salt
6 small sheets of toasted nori
handful of spinach leaves,
    stalks removed

Salmon, Spinach, and Wasabi Rolls

Use good all-purpose or mashing potatoes like Burbank or Russet Arcadia for this recipe. You want a smooth, thick mixture so the filling stays solid and rolls easily.

• Cook the potatoes in a pan of boiling salted water for 20–30 minutes, or until tender. Mash, then mix them with the scallion and enough wasabi to give the mixture a bit of a kick. Season with salt to taste. Let chill for 30 minutes, or until the mixture is very firm.

• If using the salmon fillet, pull the skin off and remove any bones. Heat the oil in a skillet and cook the salmon over medium heat, on both sides, for 8 minutes or until it is cooked through. Let cool and cut the sushi or cooked salmon into strips.

• Divide the potato, scallion, and wasabi mixture into 6 equal portions. Put a sheet of nori shiny-side down on a rolling mat with the longest end toward you and mound 1 portion of the mixture on the bottom third of the nori. Lay a sixth of the spinach leaves on top, then a layer of salmon.

• To roll the sushi, fold the mat over, starting at the end where the ingredients are, and tucking in the end of the nori to start the roll. Keep rolling, lifting up the mat as you go and keeping the pressure even but gentle until you have finished the roll. Moisten the top edge of the nori with water to seal the sushi roll closed.

• Remove the roll from the mat and cut it into 4 even-size pieces with a wet, very sharp knife. Turn the pieces on end and arrange them on a plate. Repeat with the remaining ingredients.

MAKES 24 PIECES
2 large potatoes, peeled
    and cut into quarters
2 tbsp butter
salt and pepper

1 tbsp olive oil
8 large scallops, cleaned
6 sheets of toasted nori
2 tbsp Japanese mayonnaise
2 tbsp toasted sesame seeds

Scallop, Mayonnaise, Potato, and Sesame Rolls

This recipe also works with firm white fish or salmon fillets. Use thick slices of fillet and broil or steam until it is just cooked.

• Cook the potatoes in a pan of boiling salted water for 20–30 minutes, or until tender. Mash with the butter and season well with the salt and pepper. Let chill for 30 minutes, or until the mixture is very firm.

• Heat the oil in a skillet and sauté the scallops on both sides for 2–3 minutes. Slice them thinly into 3 coin-shape pieces and season with salt to taste.

• Divide the potato mixture into 6 equal portions. Put a sheet of nori shiny-side down on a rolling mat with the longest end toward you and mound 1 portion of the potato mixture on the bottom third of the nori. Spread some mayonnaise on top, then sprinkle on some sesame seeds. Add a sixth of the scallop slices.

• To roll the sushi, fold the mat over, starting at the end where the ingredients are, and tucking in the end of the nori to start the roll. Keep rolling, lifting up the mat as you go and keeping the pressure even but gentle until you have finished the roll. Moisten the top edge of the nori with water to seal the sushi roll closed.

• Remove the roll from the mat and cut it into 4 even-size pieces with a wet, very sharp knife. Turn the pieces on end and arrange them on a plate. Repeat with the remaining ingredients.

MAKES 8 PIECES
4 aburage (deep-fried tofu sheets)
¾ cup dashi stock
3 tbsp soy sauce

2 tbsp superfine sugar
1 tbsp sake
¼ quantity freshly cooked Sushi Rice
1 tbsp toasted sesame seeds

Sushi Bags

Aburage are skins made by lifting the skin off soy milk and drying it. The pouches are used to make this inari (stuffed) sushi. Some come dry, others are preseasoned.

• Put the tofu in a bowl and pour boiling water over it to remove any excess oil, drain, and let cool. Cut each piece in half and gently open out each half into a bag.

• Mix the dashi stock, soy sauce, sugar, and sake together in a pan and bring to a boil, add the tofu bags, and let simmer for 10–15 minutes until the liquid has almost all been absorbed. Remove from the heat, drain, and let cool. Press any remaining liquid out of the bags with a clean dish towel—they should be moist but not wet.

• Add the sesame seeds to the sushi rice and mix them in. Fill the bags with the rice mixture and fold over the tops to enclose them. Serve at room temperature.

MAKES 12 PIECES

3¼ x 2½-inch/8 x 6-cm piece
  center-cut tuna fillet (ask for
  a piece ¾ inch/2 cm thick)

2 tsp sesame oil

2 tbsp toasted sesame seeds

3 small sheets of nori, cut into
  4 strips lengthwise

2 tbsp oil

Tuna Sesame Blocks

Sesame oil comes in 2 types: pale unroasted oil, usually Middle Eastern, or dark roasted oil, usually from Asia or China. The roasted oil has a much stronger flavor.

• Cut the tuna into 12 cubes and roll the cubes in the sesame oil, followed by the sesame seeds.

• Roll each cube in a sheet of nori, trimming off any excess so that the nori goes round the tuna once with only a little overlap. Moisten the edge of the nori with a little water to stick it down.

• Heat the oil in a skillet and put the cubes into the pan, standing them up on one nori-free end. Cook for 2 minutes, then turn over to cook the other nori-free end. The sesame seeds should be a dark brown, but not burned, and the tuna should have cooked most of the way through, leaving a rare patch in the center. If you prefer your tuna fully cooked, then just cook each end for a little longer.

MAKES 6–8 PIECES
8 asparagus spears
4 eggs
1 tbsp water
1 tbsp mirin
1 tsp soy sauce
½ tbsp oil

TO SERVE
Ponzu Sauce

Asparagus and Omelet Rolls with Ponzu Sauce

Ponzu Sauce is traditionally made with ponzu, or kalamansi, an Asian citron variety. Lemon or lime juice can be used instead.

• Lay the asparagus flat in a skillet filled with simmering water and cook until tender when pierced with the tip of a knife. Let cool.

• Whisk the eggs with the water, mirin, and soy sauce. Heat the oil in a nonstick skillet and pour in the egg mixture. Cook on one side until the top is just set, then add the asparagus spears by laying them in lines at one end of the skillet.

• Shake the skillet to loosen the omelet. Now roll up the omelet, starting at the asparagus end, by tipping the skillet away from you so that the omelet slides up the side of the skillet. Using 2 chopsticks, fold the omelet over and keep rolling it up like a jelly roll.

• Put a sheet of plastic wrap in the center of a rolling mat. Tip the omelet out onto the plastic wrap and roll it up in the mat to help it set in shape. Let cool.

• Remove the roll from the mat and cut it into ¾-inch/2-cm pieces with a wet, very sharp knife. Turn the pieces on end and arrange them on a plate. Serve with the Ponzu Sauce for dipping.

MAKES 12 PIECES

2 red bell peppers

1 small ripe avocado, cut into slices

8 large cooked shelled shrimp

salt and pepper

Shrimp Rolls

Avocado used for sushi should be firm and ripe, but not overripe or the pressure used to roll the sushi will squash it.

• Preheat the oven to 400°F/200°C. Put the bell peppers in a roasting pan and cook them for 30 minutes, or until the skins have browned and started to puff away from the flesh. Let cool, then pull off the skins. Cut each bell pepper in half and discard the stalk, seeds, and membrane.

• Lay out each bell pepper half on a board and make a pile of avocado slices at one end. Add 2 shrimp to each and season well with salt and pepper. Roll up the peppers tightly, wrap each roll in plastic wrap, and let chill for 30 minutes.

• Carefully unwrap the plastic wrap from the bell peppers and trim each end until it is straight. Cut each into 3 pieces with a wet, very sharp knife. Turn the pieces on end and arrange them on a plate.

SERVES 4

1 potato, peeled

¼ butternut squash, peeled

1 small sweet potato, peeled

1 small eggplant

5½ oz/150 g package tempura mix

6 green beans, trimmed

1 red bell pepper, cut into thick strips

12 oz/350 g block firm tofu, cubed

6 whole shiitake or white
    mushrooms, stalks trimmed

1 stalk broccoli, broken into florets

oil, for deep-frying

few drops of sesame oil

TO SERVE

sweet chili sauce

Vegetable and Tofu Tempura

Tofu is sold in packages in most supermarkets, but you will find a much wider variety in Japanese or Chinese stores. Silken tofu is very soft and breaks easily, but has a wonderful texture. Firm tofu is harder and easier to use. There is a Japanese version called nigari.

• Cut the potato, squash, sweet potato, and eggplant into ½-inch/1-cm thick pieces.

• Blend the tempura mix with the amount of water described on the package instructions until you have a lumpy batter full of air bubbles. Do not try to make the batter smooth or it will be heavy, and make sure you use it straightaway or it will settle.

• Drop all the prepared vegetables and tofu into the batter.

• Heat the oil in a deep-fryer to 350–375°F/180–190°C, or until a cube of bread browns in 30 seconds. Add a few drops of sesame oil.

• Add the tempura in batches of 2–3. If you add too many pieces at one time the oil temperature will drop and the batter will be soggy. When the tempura pieces are a very light golden color, which should take only 2–3 minutes, take them out, and try to drain off as much oil as possible. Let them drain on a piece of paper towel for 30 seconds to blot up more oil.

• Serve this dish very hot with sweet chili sauce.

SERVES 4

8 large raw shrimp, shelled
and deveined
4 scallops, cleaned
8 squid rings

7 oz/200 g firm white fish fillets,
cut into strips
5½ oz/150 g package tempura mix
oil, for deep-frying
few drops of sesame oil

TO SERVE

shoyu (Japanese soy sauce)

Seafood Tempura

Tempura mix is available in
packages and just needs
to be mixed with water.
Don't be tempted to make
a smooth batter because a
lumpier batter works better.

• Make little cuts on the underside of the shrimp to keep them straight while they cook. Pull any membranes off the squid rings.

• Blend the tempura mix with the amount of water described on the package instructions until you have a lumpy batter full of air bubbles. Do not try to make the batter smooth or it will be heavy, and make sure you use it straightaway or it will settle.

• Drop all the seafood into the batter.

• Heat the oil in a deep-fryer to 350–375°F/180–190°C, or until a cube of bread browns in 30 seconds. Add a few drops of sesame oil to the fryer.

• Add the tempura in batches of 2–3. If you add too many pieces at one time the oil temperature will drop and the batter will be soggy. When the tempura pieces are a very light golden color, which should take only 2–3 minutes, take them out, and try to drain off as much oil as possible. Let them drain on a piece of paper towel for 30 seconds to blot up more oil.

• Serve this dish very hot with the shoyu as a dipping sauce.

SERVES 4

4 cups water

2 teaspoons powdered dashi

6 oz/175 g block soft tofu, cut into
½-inch/1-cm cubes

4 shiitake or white mushrooms,
sliced

4 tbsp miso

2 scallions, chopped

Miso Soup

Dashi is a soup stock made from bonito flakes, kombu, and water. It is available as dashi powder and just needs to be mixed with water.

• Put the water and dashi in a pan and bring it to a boil. Add the tofu and mushrooms, turn down the heat, and let simmer gently for 3 minutes. Stir in the miso and let simmer gently until it has dissolved completely. Turn off the heat, add the scallion, and serve straightaway—the longer you leave miso the more it will settle and separate out.

Index

aburage 82
asparagus 15, 16, 86
  crab and shiitake rolls 16
  and omelet rolls 86
  salmon and mayonnaise rolls 15
avocado 12, 26, 39, 48, 64, 88
  and salmon pressed sushi 32
  shrimp and crab scattered
    sushi 46
  and shrimp skewers 24

beans, green 34, 68, 90
beef
  soy-glazed steak 45
  teriyaki, inside-out rolls 29
bell peppers, red 40, 88, 90
boat sushi (gunkanmaki) 53, 66–73
box sushi (hako-zushi) 30–41
broccoli, tempura 90

California pressed sushi 39
California rolls 12
  inside-out 26
canapés 9, 53, 75
chicken teriyaki rolls 22, 29
cocktail sushi on scallop shells 50
cod hand rolls 58
crab 12, 26, 29
  asparagus and shiitake rolls 16
  scattered sushi with shrimp
    and avocado 46
cucumber, pressed sushi with
  smoked salmon 36

daikon 42, 45
dashi stock 82, 94
drinks 75
duck and hoisin hand rolls 61

eel, glazed, hand rolls 64
eggplant, tempura 90
equipment 7, 31

ginger
  fresh 62
  pickled 9, 12, 31, 34

glazed eel hand rolls 64
green bean sushi boats 68
gunkunmaki see boat sushi

hako-zushi see box sushi
hand-rolled sushi (temaki) 52–65

inside-out rolls 26, 29

kalamansi 86
kombu 10, 94

lemon pepper crab boats 72
lobster, scattered sushi 48
lunchboxes 9

mackerel, smoked, scattered
  sushi 42
make-zushi see rolled sushi
mayonnaise
  dipping sauce 31
  Japanese 18
  lemon 32
  wasabi 48
Mediterranean pressed sushi 40
mirin 16, 22, 45, 64, 86
miso soup 75, 94
mozzarella cheese 40
mushrooms, shiitake 16, 45, 90, 94

noodles, soba 76
nori sheets 9, 24

omelet rolls, with asparagus 86
oshi waku 7, 30–41
oshi-zushi see pressed sushi

panko 21
pepper
  lemon 72
  Szechuan 56
pork tonkatsu rolls 21
pressed sushi (oshi-zushi) 31–41

rice, cooking 10
rolled sushi (make-zushi) 8–29

see also hand-rolled sushi
asparagus and omelet rolls 86
inside-out 26, 29
salmon, spinach, and wasabi
  rolls 79
scallop, mayonnaise, potato,
  and sesame rolls 80
shrimp rolls 88
soba noodle rolls 76
tuna sesame blocks 85

sake 22, 64, 75, 82
salmon 80
  asparagus and mayonnaise
    rolls 15
  inside-out teriyaki rolls 29
  roe sushi boats 67
  seven-spiced rolls 18
  smoked
    and avocado pressed
      sushi 32
    and cucumber pressed
      sushi 36
    sushi boats 70
  spinach and wasabi
    rolls 79
  sweet chili hand rolls 55
salt and pepper squid hand rolls 56
sauces
  hoisin 61
  Ponzu 16, 70, 86
  soy 9, 22, 31, 53, 64, 93
  sweet chili 55, 90
  teriyaki 22, 29, 34
scallops
  cocktail scattered sushi 50
  potato and sesame rolls 80
  seafood tempura 93
scattered sushi (chirashi-zushi) 31,
  42–51
seafood tempura 93
seaweed, nori 9, 24
seven-spiced salmon rolls 18
shiitake mushrooms 49, 90, 94
  crab and asparagus rolls 16
shoyu see soy sauce

shrimp
  and avocado skewers 24
  rolls 88
  seafood tempura 93
  with avocado and crab 46
sichimi togarashi 18
soba noodle rolls 76
soup, miso 75, 94
soy sauce 9, 22, 31, 45, 53, 64
spinach, salmon, and wasabi rolls
  79
squash, tempura 90
squid
  salt and pepper hand rolls 56
  seafood tempura 93
sweet chili salmon hand rolls 55

temaki see hand-rolled sushi
tempura 75, 90, 93
teriyaki tuna pressed sushi 34
tofu 29, 94
  and vegetable tempura 90
tofu sheets 82
tomatoes, sundried 40
tonkatsu crumbs 21
trout, smoked, sushi boats 70
tuna 72
  sesame blocks 85
  soba noodle rolls 72
  tataki hand rolls 62
  teriyaki pressed sushi 34

vegetable and tofu tempura 90

wasabi 9, 31, 39, 48, 53, 79
white fish 80
  cod hand rolls 58
  seafood tempura 93